Piano
Vocal
Guitar

SELECTIONS FROM
SENSE AND SENSIBILITY

ISBN 978-0-7935-7012-6

HAL•LEONARD®
CORPORATION
7777 W. BLUEMOUND RD. P.O. BOX 13819 MILWAUKEE, WI 53213

WEEP YOU NO MORE SAD FOUNTAINS

By PATRICK DOYLE

Weep you no more sad — foun - tains; what _____ need you flow so

fast? Look how the snow - y _____

moun - tains heav - en's sun doth gen - tly _____

waste. But _____ my sun's _____

heav - en - ly eyes view not your

4

weep - ing that now lies sleep - ing soft - ly,

soft - ly, now _____ soft - ly, soft - ly

lies _____ sleep - ing.

sleep - ing.

THE DREAME

By PATRICK DOYLE

HL00351324

SONY PICTURES MUSIC GROUP

EXCLUSIVELY DISTRIBUTED BY

HAL•LEONARD® CORPORATION

7777 W. BLUEMOUND RD. P.O. BOX 13819 MILWAUKEE, WI 53213

ISBN-13: 978-0-7935-7012-6

Distributed By

HAL LEONARD

00351324

9 780793 570126

U.S. $12.99